CHINA DOLL

CHINA DOLL

A PLAY BY

David Mamet

THEATRE COMMUNICATIONS GROUP / NEW YORK / 2015

China Doll is published by Theatre Communications Group, Inc., 520 Eighth Avenue, 24th Floor, New York, NY 10018-4156

The publication of *China Doll* by David Mamet, through TCG's Book Program, is made possible in part by the New York State Council on the Arts with the support of Governor Andrew Cuomo and the New York State Legislature.

TCG books are exclusively distributed to the book trade by Consortium Book Sales and Distribution.

Cataloging-in-Publication Data is on file at the Library of Congress, Washington, DC.

ISBN 978-1-55936-502-4 (paperback)
ISBN 978-1-55936-831-5 (ebook)

Book design and composition by Lisa Govan
Cover design by Serino/Coyne

First Edition, November 2015

This play is dedicated to Al Pacino

CHINA DOLL

PRODUCTION HISTORY

China Doll had its world premiere on Broadway at the Gerald Schoenfeld Theatre on November 19, 2015. It was directed by Pam MacKinnon. The scenic design was by Derek McLane, the costume design was by Jess Goldstein, the lighting design was by Russell H. Champa and the sound design was by Peter Fitzgerald. The cast was:

MICKEY ROSS	Al Pacino
CARSON	Christopher Denham

CHARACTERS

MICKEY ROSS, an older man
CARSON, a younger man

SCENE

An apartment

One: Evening
Two: Morning

She drawled so sweetly and fixed her mouth in such an odd way that he was impelled to kiss her. "You clover blossom," he would say to her, coming over and taking her by the arms. "You sprig of cherry bloom. You Dresden china dream."

—THEODORE DREISER, *THE TITAN*

ONE

The apartment. Evening.
Mickey Ross is seated at a table by a telephone. Beat. There is a knock at the door.

MICKEY: *Come* in.

(*Carson enters, carrying a folded newspaper, which he extends toward Mickey.*)

What is that? A newspaper. I don't want a "newspaper." What do I want?

CARSON: Sir?

MICKEY: . . . you *come* here, what the hell do you *come* here for? I've got a sheaf of letters *testifying* to your . . .

CARSON: . . . sir.

MICKEY: . . . your various great virtues, but I ask you to perform one simple task . . . What was that?

(Pause.)

I asked you a question.

CARSON: . . . I.

MICKEY: What did I ask you to do?

CARSON: . . . sir.

MICKEY: To find out where Ms. Pierson is.

CARSON: Ms. Pierson is in the hotel.

(Carson hands the newspaper to Mickey.)

MICKEY: I *called* the . . . *(He bats the newspaper away)* I don't want the fucking newspaper. I want you to do what I'm paying you for. Where is Ms. Pierson?

CARSON: In *Toronto*, in the ho—

MICKEY: Did I tell you I just *called*? The *plane* is in Toronto, is that corr . . . ?

CARSON: That's right.

MICKEY: Because you *told* me she went from the plane to *where*?

CARSON: The Choate Hotel.

MICKEY: She's not there. And find me the pilot.

CARSON: His cell phone doesn't ans—

MICKEY: Get me Flight Services. In Toronto. You have the tail number? *(He checks a note)* It's CH-134.

CARSON: That's not the . . .

MICKEY: Just . . .

CARSON: "CH" . . . that's the *Swiss* registration, sir, the plane has a U.S. registration, the number is—

MICKEY: Get me Flight Services in Toronto.

(Carson makes a call on a second phone.)

And the plane does not have the U.S. registration. It has the *Swiss* registr . . . What the *fuck* am I *paying* you for?

CARSON *(On the second phone)*: Yes. I'm calling about . . . tail number, November, 241 Mike Alpha. A *Mark Five*.

MICKEY *(To Carson)*: That's a U.S. registration. The plane is registered in *Switzerland* . . .

CARSON *(Holds up a finger)*: I'm sorry, sir . . .

(He checks the invoice.)

MICKEY: Let's start anew . . . the plane *is* in Toronto?

(Pause.)

CARSON: I . . .

MICKEY: The pilot. Closed the *flight* plan. I was *told* the plane therefore had landed in Toronto. Is that true?

CARSON *(Into phone)*: . . . Hello . . . ?

(Mickey takes the phone from him.)

MICKEY *(Into phone)*: Yes. Hello. Who am I speaking to? This is Mickey Ross. Yes. Mickey Ross. We do a lot of business with you folks. I'm looking for: tail number . . .

(He checks a piece of paper.)

(Into phone; reading paper) CH-134

(Pause.)

It's the new Mark Five.

(Pause.)

Aerstar Mark Five. You're only going to have one on the ramp.

(Pause.)

You do.

(Pause.)

Well, what *is* the tail number?

(Mickey writes it down.)

(Into phone) November 241 Mike Alpha. That's the wrong num . . . I've got a sixty-million-dollar airplane on your ramp and it's a Chinese *fire* drill up there. Do you know how much business I do with you?

(Pause.)

Let me talk to the pilot. Aerstar's ferry pilot. Is he there?

(Pause.)

Did he leave a *contact* number?

(Pause.)

Please give it to me . . . It's *my plane.* Call Aerstar. In Switzerland, they will verify . . . Never mind.

(Pause.)

When the pilot checks in. Tell him to call his employer. And what is *your* name?

(Pause. Mickey writes down the information.)

And *what* is your position there? . . . Thank you.

(He hangs up.)

CARSON: Mr. Ross . . .

MICKEY: You know, I can't spend my time wondering: "Do those in my employ *appreciate* my desires." You are not getting paid to do that. But to *fulfill* them. Which, in this case, were, to *arrange* for Ms. Pierson and me to . . .

CARSON: Sir.

MICKEY: . . . rendezvous in Toronto and continue on to *London. On* the new plane. *That's* all.

CARSON: Sir.

MICKEY: And all of this *nonsense* about how you very much admire me; and all this bow-tied bullshit . . .

(Carson starts to speak.)

You think I'm a *fool?* To enjoy your deference? You want someone to praise you? Do as you're fucking told. One thing I asked: to treat my friend with care. *She* is in an exposed position. What does she require of me? *Protection.* That's not an empty word, Mr. *Carson?* Evil minds might say "she went with him for his money." That's *correct.* She *did.* As *money* means *protection,* which she requires, and which I am *thrilled* to be able to provide. And which job I delegated to *you.*

(Pause.)

Have I treated you with anything but respect since you have worked for me? Answer me.

(Pause.)

CARSON: No, sir.

(The phone rings.)

MICKEY: But you find these errands "beneath you"?
CARSON: I . . .
MICKEY: With your fucking "credentials" . . . Get the phone.

(Carson does so.)

CARSON *(Into phone)*: Hello . . . ? *(Pause. To Mickey)* It's your
attorney.

(Mickey takes the phone.)

MICKEY *(Into phone)*: Yes. *Henry. (Pause. To Carson)* "The plane *is*
in Toronto." *(Into phone)* . . . What about the tail num . . . ?
"The Swiss Changed the Tail Number."

(Pause.)

Why?

(Pause.)

As a "*courtesy*"? *Who* said that? "Aerstar"? That's swell.
They gave it a U.S. registration, but it's still a Swiss plane
till I accept it. Isn't that the case? Swiss registry, we keep
it, based out of the country, six months, and we pay no
sales tax. Isn't that corr . . . *What?*

(Pause.)

No. We don't owe any sales tax. What are they talking
ab . . . ?

(Pause.)

. . . Because it touched down *in state*? With a U.S. registration? I'm not paying five million in sales ttt . . . Look Aerstar? The *tax* thing? That's the *dodge*, everybody here had to tack on the vigorish, Aerstar couldn't sell a *plane*. Wh . . . who's going to spend five million dollars on sales tax if he can legally avoid it? *Why?* So the Kid can buy votes and play *Dollhouse*? We owe them no sales tax. And I sent Frankie, who, all right, is a British National, on *Company Business*, from Saint-Estèphe, which, you will allow, is not in the United States, to Toronto, where I am to meet her, avoiding the U.S. *specifically*, to be in compliance with the state *tax* law, and you tell that fool at Aerstar, he wants to fuck with me I'll give 'im the plane back, and he's going home by *weeping cross*. It's a Brit expression. I got it from Frankie. Yeah, she's *full* of charm.

(Pause.)

I *think* she's well . . . She may be somewhere, in *Canada* . . . it seems we don't *know*. *(Turns to Carson, who has motioned to him) What?*

CARSON: Ms. Pierson's in the Choate Hotel, sir.

MICKEY: Ms. Pierson's *not* in the hotel.

CARSON: She's registered under a false name.

MICKEY *(Into phone)*: Henry—I'll call you back. *(He hangs up)* What?

CARSON: Ms. Pierson is registered. At the hotel. Under a false name.

MICKEY: Why would she do that?

CARSON: Sir, I don't know.

(Pause.)

MICKEY: She's in the hotel in Toronto.
CARSON: Yes.
MICKEY: How did you find out?
CARSON: I called the hotel concierge. And described her.

(Pause.)

MICKEY: And is that what you were trying to tell me?
CARSON: Yes, sir.

(Pause.)

MICKEY: What name is she staying under?
CARSON: Ann Black.

(Pause.)

MICKEY: Well— Look what I've done.

(Pause.)

Carson, I most humbly beg your pardon.
CARSON: That's all right, sir.
MICKEY: No. It's not. There's no excuse for me to treat you
that way.
CARSON: Sir . . .
MICKEY: You have a difficult job. And I am *grateful* to you. For
doing it with *discretion*. For which my arrogance is cruel
repayment. And I am *most* heartily ashamed of my behav-
ior. Well, it has a name. The Name. For the behavior is
"An Old Man's Love."

(Pause.)

Which cannot excuse, but may perhaps explain my disgraceful outburst. A beautiful *woman* . . .

CARSON: Sir, you owe me no explanation.
MICKEY: Please.

(Pause.)

A beautiful woman will never be alone. As she requires protection. Men *pursue* her, and she will accept the best current offer. She must *protect* herself, as all compete for her. And will plague her. Until she declares an alliance. In this competition, might I offer a preemptive bid? Yes. Is it youth or beauty? No. It's wealth. Should I berate myself for having wealth? Should she for having *beauty?* Who would say so? I . . .
CARSON: Mr. Ross . . .
MICKEY: Allow me to perform my penance.

(Pause.)

I am not insensible. That some might say: the old man bought her. *Fine.* People may envy me, as well they *should.* But Ms. Pierson was going to accept someone. She could have had any man she wished. She chose *me.* She's welcome to whatever I have. I only wish I could do more.
CARSON: If I may, sir, you give her everything she wants.
MICKEY: But I don't give her everything I want. You understand? I love her. There it is . . . And, after a certain point. What can I offer her but thoughtfulness?

(Pause.)

The Old Man taught that if we are unsure of our faults, we should atone for our virtues—I pride myself on being *fair.* But I berated you, which was both unfair and thoughtless. And I'm truly sorry.

CARSON: I assure you, the incident's forgotten.

MICKEY: I very much appreciate it, Carson. And I won't forget it. Thank you.

CARSON: Sir, you're welcome.

MICKEY: That's an admirable trait.

CARSON: What is?

MICKEY: To allow someone to apologize.

(Pause.)

Well.

(Pause.)

Would you please get me the manager of the hotel in Toronto?

(Carson dials.)

What name is she staying under?

CARSON *(To Mickey)*: Ann Black. *(Into phone)* One moment . . .

(Mickey gestures and Carson hands him the phone.)

MICKEY *(Into phone)*: Yes? I'd like to speak to a Miss Ann *Black*. Is she register . . . *(To Carson)* Thank you . . .

CARSON: You're wel . . .

MICKEY *(Into phone)*: Please put me th . . . Why not?

(Pause.)

Of *course* she has a "Do Not Dis . . ." But would you put the call through? It's quite important . . .

(Pause.)

Then please give me the manager.

(Pause. The other phone rings. Carson picks it up.)

Yes I'll hold.

CARSON *(Into phone)*: . . . Yes . . . ?

MICKEY *(To Carson)*: Who is it?

CARSON *(To Mickey)*: Your attorney.

MICKEY *(To Carson)*: Give it to me.

(Carson takes the first phone from Mickey; into the other phone:)

Henry. *Hello.* The tax issue? Let it ride. No, I can't talk now. Al . . . *Henry.* What?

(Pause.)

They're "holding" the plane? What do you mean? *They?* Who is "*they*"? The Canadians. Are "holding my *plane*"? *Why?* "*Taxes* . . . ?" There *are* no Canadian ttt . . . "The state *sales* tax"? *Here?* THE PLANE. Touched down here with a *warning* light. *(Looks at Carson who nods; into phone)* *That's* why it touched down in the states. Their pilot declared an emergency.

(Pause.)

Well, you tell *me.*

(Pause.)

"The Pilot Had No Choice." What is it?

CARSON: International law.
MICKEY: It's an "aircraft in dist . . ."?

(Pause.)

Well, then, why are the Canadians holding my pl . . . A request from *whom? (To Carson)* Our State Franchise Tax Board—*why? (Repeating Henry)* "Because of the U.S. tail number." *(Pause. Into phone)* How, how can it be an "attempt to evade tax . . ." I don't even *own* the plane yet. I haven't *accepted* it. It's on a delivery flight fr . . . *I* didn't put the U.S. tail number *on* it. *Aerstar* did. I gave them a deposit, and I'll cancel the *order.* Why in the *world* would the Canadians . . . "They got a request to impound my plane as a lien against taxes." That's, that's absurd. I assume the request is from our governor.

(Pause.)

Well, where else would the request "issue" from?

(Pause.)

All right . . . "Taking a deep breath." It's a pro-forma claim, made by the state, we'll work it out in tax court. And if the state thinks I owe the tax, let them give me a *bill.* Maybe I'll pay it. And let's get *on* with it. I'm going on a *trip* . . .

(Pause.)

What?

(Pause.)

"The plane can't fly."

(Pause.)

All right: It can't fly until *what*? "Until the tax matter's *adjudicated*"? That's *absurd*. Where, where is *that* written?

CARSON *(Into second phone)*: One moment please for Mr. Ross. *(To Mickey)* James Price, manager of the Choate Hotel, Toronto.

MICKEY *(Into his phone)*: Henry. Work it out. *They* can't hold the plane in *Canada* on a U.S. *tax*. How can they hold the plane, on a U.S. *tax* matter. *(To Carson)* Get me in touch with Aerstar. The Mark Five. What's the salesman's name?

CARSON: Brandt. Aerstar, U.S.

MICKEY: *What's* the guy's name?

CARSON: Frederick Brandt. *(Into phone)* Mr. Ross will be right with you, sir. Thank you for waiting.

MICKEY *(Into his phone)*: Henry. It may be they're going to want to throw their hands up. But it's their plane. Aerstar. The state wants to stick us with the tax bill, end of the day. Let Aerstar work it out, *pay* it, or we'll walk away from the deal. More *importantly*? Why are they picking on me? "Have I made anyone mad?"

(Pause.)

I'll call you back. *(Hangs up. To Carson)* I need to talk to Rubenstein.

CARSON *(Referring to phone; sotto voce)*: The hotel manager.

(Mickey takes the phone from Carson.)

MICKEY *(Into phone)*: Hello? *(To Carson)* Get me Dave Rubenstein. *(Into phone)* Mr. . . . .

(Carson hands him a card.)

Price. This is Mickey Ross. Yes. Mickey Ross. A *friend* is staying in your hotel. *(To Carson) What* name is she under?

CARSON: Ann . . .

(Carson dials second phone.)

MICKEY *(Into phone)*: Under the name of Miss Ann Black. "She has a 'Do Not Disturb' on her line." But it's essential that I speak to her. Could you please put me through? It's quite important.

(Pause.)

She's a friend of mine.

(Pause.)

"She's not picking up the phone." Mr., Mr. *Price*, she *is* in your hotel? . . . You're *sure* . . .

(Pause.)

Ah. "They brought her some room service." What'd she eat?

(Pause.)

Excellent. Yes, no. Well, we'll let her sleep. I just wanted to be sure she was tucked in and taken care of, and I see that she is. Thank you.

(Pause.)

Not at all. Not at all, Mr. Price. Thank you.

(He hangs up.)

CARSON *(Into his phone)*: Yes?
MICKEY: Rubenstein?
CARSON: Frederick Brandt, Aerstar, U.S.

(Mickey takes the phone.)

MICKEY *(Into phone)*: *Frederick.*

(Pause.)

Thank you for calling. The . . . the *gift*? Yes, what gift?

(Mickey looks at Carson, who shrugs. Carson picks up the other phone and speaks into it, sotto voce.)

(Into phone) It *may* be here. I. *Frederick* . . . What? "The plane is fine." That's *reassuring*. "Just a warning light." "It was not an actual emergency . . ." Fine, but your pilot *declared* an emergency . . . ?

(Pause.)

Well, what other test would there be? Look. Your plane. Has been *detained* and, it seems, *impounded*. In Toronto.
CARSON *(Covers his phone)*: There *is* a package. Shall they bring it in?
MICKEY *(To Carson)*: No, please go get it.

(Carson hangs up, then exits.)

(Into phone) . . . It is being *held* because of a U.S. *tax* iss . . . Frederick, why did you paint the U.S. registration number on the plane? "A courtesy." No, the courtesy is lovely. Had the plane not touched down in *state*, as now there's a *tax* iss . . . I'm not *saying* it's your fault—I'm saying it's your *problem*.

(Pause.)

Yes, it *will* be sorted out, as shall most things. But, at this hour: you have my *deposit*, Canada has *your plane*. My state wants five million dollars in tax, and the green grass grew all around, all around.

(Pause.)

No. *Your* plane, Frederick, not *mine*.

(Pause.)

Indeed, but the contract, I presume, specified "airworthy." Was that not included in the purchase price?

(Pause.)

Yes. The plane *may* have been safe. But . . .

(Pause.)

"One simple fuel light." That may be the case, but the pilot *declared* an emergency . . . Does that go on the plane's various logs? Its "flight log," and so on?

(Pause.)

You want to add greater redundancies. That's fine. And the cost of those redundancies will, I am sure, be borne by the plane's eventual purchaser, whomever that may be.

I would have *thought* the price included an operative warning light, as I'd hate to think you folks were cutting corners. At that price . . .

(Pause.)

"The increased costs of the interior." "And the permitting . . ." Wait, the "*permitting* process"— didn't I *pay* for that? . . . *(Covers phone; to himself)* "As Ms. Pierson utilized the costliest material and components in its design." "And we'd hate, when she was going to be working for Aerstar, to begin the associ . . ." *(Into phone)* All right, after the Patty-Cake. Pal, *look*, should it occur there are artistic differences between Ms. Pierson and your company, she will, no doubt, find other means to pass the time. For example, designing the interior of whatever plane I eventually buy, having rejected yours . . .

(Carson enters carrying a large gift-wrapped box. Mickey gestures to Carson to undo the wrapping. Carson does so.)

(Into phone) . . . and *you* having refunded my deposit. Plus whatever *damages* . . . Well, perhaps I *misheard* you, but you *seemed* to say the plane was not *air-worthy*, as you skimped on the warning system, to spruce up the interior. Which, I believe I was *paying* fff . . .

(Pause.)

That's *not* what you're saying? Good, as that, of course, would do havoc to your reputa . . . And to your ability to sell planes here in the United States.

(Pause.)

I simply wondered why you chose to mention *the interior*.
Oh, good. So we're all *friends*. And you intended nothing.
That's swell . . . Oh, and here's your *gift*!

(Carson takes a model of a large business jet out of the box.)

(Into phone) Well, look at *that* . . . That's beautiful. It's
made of "*metal . . .*"

(Pause.)

"The same steel and aluminum as the plane *itself* . . ."

(Mickey gestures to Carson, who hands him the plane.)

(Into phone) It's got the same *paint* scheme, it's got the
same unfortunate U.S. *tail* number . . . And—what—it
does *tricks*?

(Mickey starts manipulating the plane.)

(Into phone) . . . How do you open it? . . . Ah.

*(The top of the fuselage comes off, revealing a plush interior in
beige leather.)*

(Into phone) ". . . And she did the *interior*." *(To Carson)* "It's
exactly the interior designed by Ms. Pierson." . . . The
card?

(Mickey takes the card and reads it:)

"Looking forward to working with Ms. Pierson." *(Into phone)* She's going to be very flattered. She's looking forward to working with you, too. I know.

(Pause.)

Thank you. I do, too, but then I'm prejudiced.

(Pause.)

Well, I hope that she *is* working for you. 'Cause I suspect you'd rather see a lot of *her* than a lot of *me*.

(Pause.)

It doesn't *need* a fine-tooth comb, Frederick. I'm sure all that's required's a new warning light, but, we'll *see*. Thank you for the gift. I'm sure the *actual* plane's lovely, too. Sitting there in Canada. Unable to move.

(Pause.)

I *believe* because, of a request by our *governor*. But, here's what: *Frederick?* I'm . . . I am going to work the tax matter out with the state and, it may be, when the dust clears, perhaps, we'll have another talk. *(To Carson)* "It will be easy as Ms. Pierson will be working for him." *(Into phone)* All right. Let's leave it at that.

(Mickey picks up a newspaper and reads. Then he speaks into the phone:)

. . . We're not sure of our travel plans, just now, but, when we are . . .

(Pause.)

Well, that's very generous of you. *(To Carson)* He wants to *lend* us a plane. *(Into phone)* Thank you. No, I'll *certainly* consider it.

(Pause.)

It's been good talking to you, too.

(He hangs up.)

Book me, commercial to London. And Ms. Pierson *Toronto* to London. Commercial tomorrow, noonish.

CARSON: . . . commercial.

MICKEY: Call Jimmy, have him meet her at Heathrow. Have Mrs. Sims warm up the flat.

CARSON: Didn't they offer you one of their planes?

MICKEY: Oh, yes. Would you like a "lesson"?

CARSON: Sir, I would.

MICKEY: Aerstar. Sells their planes, either with a Swiss registry, or with that of the *country of purchase*. With the Swiss number. I don't have to register it in-state for six months. *If* I keep it out of the state, I save the sales tax. They changed the tail number, that's a mistake—all right *but* it's also five million bucks somebody's liable for. *I* ain't gonna pay it. *This* fella, wants to lend me *his* plane, to fly Toronto-London. What would that cost them? In fuel?

CARSON: Eighteen, twent—?

MICKEY: Twenty grand? To save themselves five mil? No thanks, we'll fly commercial. What am I *telling* him?

CARSON: You're telling him: "Go to Hell."

MICKEY: That's correct. *(Referring to the model plane)* And what does *this* little trinket mean?

CARSON: Must it have a meaning?

MICKEY: Oh, I think everything has a "meaning." Why did they send this to me now?

CARSON: To . . . to "commemorate . . ."

MICKEY: To *commemorate* what? They haven't delivered the plane, I haven't accepted it, they had this made to give me *on* acceptance. Why do they send it to me now?

CARSON: Because the sale's in question.

MICKEY: That's right. That's all. So, *now*, what does it reveal? Is it a strong move, or a weak one?

CARSON: It's a *weak* move.

MICKEY: Why?

CARSON: Because it's transparent.

MICKEY: *That's* right. Press Aerstar to pay the tax, and they'll withdraw their offer of Ms. Pierson's job. The wiser man. Would know I know that, and refrain from the obvious threat. So they are weak. Thus, that attack is, in effect, a subconscious signal of surrender.

CARSON: If they know they're beaten, why put up a fight?

MICKEY: Oh, you got room for more wisdom?

CARSON: Please.

MICKEY: All right.

(Pause.)

Men, faced with aggression, if they do not fight, may turn subservient. That man, however, should he regain the upper hand, will strike back *savagely* at those who saw him weak. Why risk that? When you beat someone, let him keep his self-respect.

CARSON: How do you do that?

MICKEY: By displaying *such* overwhelming force that, not only your opponent, but all observers recognize: that there was no shame in surrender.

(Pause.)

Like a woman. In a seduction. To protect her reputation. That's how you do business.

CARSON: We should think of business as a sexual transaction? . . .

MICKEY: Only if you want to get rich. The Old Man taught me that. *(Referring to the newspaper)* Oh, look here: *(Reads)* "My father, the American values of Hard Work and Perseverance, which I learned from him. If I can be a fraction as brave. In my devotion to the simple truths . . ." *(To himself)* Fuckin' *Kid* . . .

(The phone rings.)

CARSON *(Into phone)*: Yes. *(To Mickey)* Mr. Rubenstein.

MICKEY: Him or his girl?

CARSON *(Shakes his head. Into phone)*: Yes, I have Mr. Ross. Please put Mr. Rubenstein on.

MICKEY: So what's the *real* threat? To Aerstar?

CARSON: Pay the sales tax or lose the sale.

MICKEY: No. The *real* threat is I announce I have canceled acceptance of their new model. For *reasons of safety.*

CARSON: They'll say it's libel.

MICKEY: Their pilot. Declared an emergency. Matter of federal record. Then what does Aerstar do, in reply?

CARSON: They cancel Ms. Pierson's job.

MICKEY: I get her another job. Chess and checkers. My move, *your* move—that's all there is. Eh? What else is there?

CARSON: Thank you for the lesson.

MICKEY: . . . What the hell . . .

(Carson hands Mickey the phone.)

(Into phone) Ruby. How are ya? Well, I bought a new plane.

(Pause.)

The *old* one? The ashtrays were full. I gave it to the Salvation Army.

(Pause.)

The *new* one? Has more "*range.*"

(Pause.)

I bought it for *Frankie.*

(Pause.)

She wants "more range." To go traveling.

(Pause.)

Don't *know*, don't care.

(Pause.)

"Likes" it? She *loves* it. "Why?" It's *shiny*. Here's the thing: new plane. Okay. Swiss registry? . . . The plane. Factory-new, from Aerstar. Pilot, en route from Saint-Estèphe to *Toronto*, forty-two-thousand feet. Fuel-warning light goes on, all he knows, he's flying a glider. He's got to put the plane down. Puts it down *here*. Guess what your *pal* wants?

(Pause.)

The *Kid.*

(Pause.)

No, Ruby, for chrissake, I'm speaking *figuratively*. His *tax* . . . the state *tax* board.

(Pause.)

Five-million-dollars sales tax.

(Pause.)

'Cause the plane touched down in state. Yes. It flew *on* to Toronto, but it "touched down" here. Now the state *tax* board . . .

(Pause.)

God fo . . . Ruby, kidding as . . . kidding aside, God forbid. The . . . the tax issue. It's only money. We'll work that out.

(Pause.)

Well, here it *is*: they've impounded the plane.

(Pause.)

The Canadians.

(Pause.)

It *is* a foreign plane. But *Aerstar*—

(The other phone rings. Carson answers it.)

CARSON *(Into phone)*: Yes?

(He listens.)

MICKEY *(To Carson)*: Ms. Pierson?

(Carson shakes his head no. Mickey picks up the model plane and looks at it. He gestures to Carson to take a message. Carson nods, does so, and hangs up the phone.)

(Into phone) Some "Swiss" painted the U.S. tail numbers on it.

(Pause.)

Fuck do I know. In an "excess of zeal." Now the state wants five million bucks in tax. They've impounded the plane. In *Toronto*.

(Pause.)

In response . . .

(He looks at Carson, who nods.)

(Into phone) To a request forwarded . . .

(Carson shrugs.)

(Into phone) To keep the plane as . . . "A lien against *taxes*"? Is this, a *glitch*? Or, is somebody tryin' to *screw* with me? Either way, *I'm* a big boy. Could you just *tell* me.

(Pause.)

I'm not *saying* it's you. I'm only asking for your *help* to *determine* . . .

(Pause.)

Why would that be *illegal*? Yes, I *can* pay the tax, but why *should* I pay the tax? If I don't *owe* . . . if I *owe* the tax, of course, I'll . . .

(Pause.)

All I'm asking is: I'd like to use the *plane*.

(Pause.)

Well, tell 'em to send me a *bill* and we'll work it out. Could you have your people look at it.

(Pause.)

"Special treatment." Oh, come *on*. Why would you, either, or the Kid, offer me special treatment? Ruby? I'm on the other sss . . . All I'm asking, is the same attention you might give to any taxpayer, our *fair state*.

(Pause.)

Dave, *you* know, I wanted to. I'd pull up stakes and move down to the islands. I'm here out of choice, and I pay every cent in taxes . . . Look, Dave, the plane, okay, you could say it's a *wedding* present.

(Pause.)

Yeah, thank you. And it goes with a sort of *vacation*.

(Pause.)

There's an old-fashioned word. *(Covers phone; to Carson)* "Honeymoon." *(Into phone)* So here we are: my plane's in hock, and can you reach out and just tell me what's *happening*? I truly appreciate it. How's the Kid?

(Pause.)

Yeah. He's a *nice clean-living kid*. And he's more fun than a Swiss army knife. "Politics"? Took to it like a preacher's son to vice. God bless him. Now, what can I do for you? What does the *Kid* need? *(To Carson)* "Money and an Issue." *(Into phone)* The *issue*, I can't help him with. The *money*? I gave in the *primary*. And I *will* give, the *general*.

(Pause.)

The *maximum allowed by law*. What is that? "Two and a half grand."

(Pause.)

Course I don't want him to win.

(Pause.)

'Cause I know how to add. But I want him to run. And I wish him well. *(Referring to the newspaper)* I see he's . . . what *is* he? . . . "Striving to find his *voice*"? And "gaining strength from his *constituents*" . . . to "tap the wisdom of the *common people*"? *(Laughs)* How *is* he? "Stressed-out."

(Pause.)

Well, I'd *think*.

(Pause.)

I remember.

(Pause.)

Not that long ago.

(Pause.)

Doesn't it? The Old Man . . . ? Drink or two by the *field-stone fireplace.*

(Pause.)

Currier and Ives . . . I swear to God . . . I'm *proud* of him, the Kid. The Old Man would be, *too.* The little skeezix. Running for the hotseat. Give him my best, and I mean it.

(Pause.)

Just to "*look into it.*" I'd appreciate it, Ruby. Thank you.

(He hangs up.)

CARSON *(Reading from his notes)*: A maid went in her room. Ms. Pierson is sleeping. She left a note for Ms. Pierson to call you.
MICKEY: Good. Let her sleep. I want you to find out who did it.
CARSON: Who did what, sir?
MICKEY: Impounded the plane.
CARSON: The *Canadians* impounded the plane.
MICKEY: Oh, *really?* In response to what? The "phases of the moon"?

(The phone rings. Carson picks it up.)

CARSON *(Into phone)*: Yes?

(He hands the phone to Mickey.)

MICKEY *(Into phone)*: Yes? *Francy. "Francine."* How are things in the Frozen North? Look, before I forget, I'm going to fly you commercial to Lon . . . Oh, "We don't fly commerc . ." Wait: didn't I find you in the gutter? Hey, France . . . didn't I put your first pair of shoes on your feet? When you were selling matches in Trafalgar Square. Covered in rags. Who . . . wait a minute, I took you in the *shift that you stood up in*, girl, and don't you forget it, or I'll give you back to the gypsies. I saved the receipt.

(Pause.)

You're flying commercial as the government, for technical reasons . . . Immm . . . what would it have to do with Immigration? Frankie? *Customs*, or some damned thing, is keeping the plane for a tax matter. It has nothing to do with imm . . .

(Pause.)

Naa, the governor's just screwing around with me.

(Pause.)

Because he *can*.

(Pause.)

I do and I *did*. Since he was a *child*.

(Pause.)

I don't know. He's on a "vision quest . . ." Carson is booking you to London. Jimmy will meet you at Heathrow, and I'll see you at the flat . . . *(To Carson)* Book me a seat . . . *(Into phone)* Were you *scared?* When the *plane diverted? (He laughs. To Carson)* She was *asleep* . . . *(Into phone)* France, why the hell did you change your *name* . . . ? Why, why are you under a false . . . Was there pr . . . was there *press?* At the airp . . .

(Pause.)

No, all right, tell me *later*, I underst . . . Hey, they sent me a model of the plane. Aerstar. Hold on: with your *interior*. Yeah, *you* saw the real thing, but *this* is my first exposure. Look here: the *top* comes off, you can see: your paint scheme, the *seats*. The same leath— Baby, it's gorgeous. And whatsisname said how they were looking forward to working with you.

(Pause.)

You go, fly with the poor people, and I'll see you at the . . . The green card? No, I *told* you, there's no . . . What would it have to do with your green card?

(Pause.)

Well, that's why we're going back to Lon . . . There is no problem with your green . . . No, hold on. Let me *finish*. Baby, you're just *tired*. Of *course* you are.

(Pause.)

Just like the "Tired and Poor." Well, ain't *you* well read. And I thought you were just a pretty face, and "rich girl shoulders." And that baby-doll porcelain *skin* . . . You want the whole *list*? . . . I got it written down.

(Pause.)

I love you ttt . . . there's . . . *Francine*: there's no immigration problem. Did you get off the pl . . . Did you get off the plane?

(Pause.)

Then there's no . . . Listen: you got spooked. And, you're over-tired . . . Because you *get* this way when you're tired. You got the *heebie-jeebies*. Now your mind's racing. Take a sl . . . Oh, okay then. What woke you up? You . . . What are you worried ab . . . *(He looks at his watch)* The *paper*? Baby—since when do you read the ppp . . .

(Pause.)

You saw it on . . . ?

(He gestures to Carson to pull it up on a tablet. Carson does so.)

(Into phone) What were you doing *online*? *Shopping?* . . . *Bet* you were shopping, what'd you buy?

(Carson shows him the item on the tablet.)

(Into phone) Hold, Frankie, hold on. *(Pause. He reads)* "After an unscheduled st . . . continued to Toronto. On board, a young woman who claimed to be Mr. Ross's fiancée . . ."

(Pause.)

"Who *claimed* to be his fiancée."

(Pause.)

Uh-huh. No. That is not polite.

(Pause.)

No. I agree with you. It's unwarranted and insulting. No. You're not overstating it. Look, look: you and I. Wherever we go. Are going to arouse. A certain amount of envy. It's inevit . . .

(Pause.)

Frank, Frankie, go look in the mirror.

(Pause.)

Who would not envy you? Or me for your companionship?

(Pause.)

Yes, they're striking at me, through you. That's absolutely right.

(Pause.)

Well, one has to learn some philosophy. We'll sit on a beach and study it. What do you say? . . .

(Pause.)

France, what are you concerned about?

(Pause.)

"You lied."

(Pause.)

When did you "lie"?

(Pause.)

When you said you didn't get off the plane. Okay. Don't worrr . . . *If* it constitutes reentry, we'll set the clock back and stay out of the country for six months. Is that it?

(Pause.)

Then what is it?

(Pause.)

Well, you have to tell me, and you're going to tell me, so, whatever it is . . .

(Pause.)

What do you mean "They *took* you off the plane"? *Who* took you off the plane?

(Pause.)

"And then . . ."?

(Pause.)

I know there's "and then," because I hear it in your voice. What is it?

(Pause.)

No.

(Pause.)

Oh no.

(Pause.)

No. They didn't.

(Pause. He gestures to Carson for a pad and a pen. Carson passes them to him.)

(Pause. Into phone) Can you tell me what uniforms they wore?

(Pause.)

Because I need to know who they were.

(Pause.)

That "*you* did something wrong"? My God. Frankie. Oh my God.

(Pause.)

I have to call you back.

(Pause.)

Because I need to find out who did this to you.

(Pause.)

Uh-huh . . . Well, you let that be my business. Can you do that?

(Pause.)

Good. You just let me take care of it. I love you, baby. And I'll call you back.

(Pause.)

Francie? I'm so very sorry. I'm so sorry.

(He hangs up the phone.)

Get me Mr. Rubenstein.

(Carson dials the phone.)

And then get back to Aerstar. Thank them. And I *will* accept their offer of the loaner plane. And get me out of here.

CARSON *(Into phone)*: Mr. Ross, for Mr. Rubenstein.

MICKEY: Toronto and then London, with Ms. Pierson.

CARSON: Now?

MICKEY: Give me the phone.

CARSON *(Into phone)*: One moment, please, for Mr. Ross . . .

MICKEY *(To himself)*: . . . This sick little *punk* . . .

(He takes the phone.)

(Into phone) Dave. Okay, I been around a long time. *As* have you. But this fuckin' *Kid.* Are you *kiddin'* me?

(Pause.)

What? My *friend* . . . Ms. *Pierson.* Was detained. At the airport. By your people, who . . . "How do I know that they're your people?" I'll *tell* you how I know, as, we find . . . *(Reading from his tablet)* "Who *claimed* to be his fiancée . . ." Where and to whom was that said, Dave? So that it's leaked in the newspapers? To whom was it said? *To your people* . . . At the airport. Uh-huh. Well. Look into this. My fiancée, a young woman, *is taken from the plane*, TAKEN OFF THE PLANE, and *strip-searched*, and *strip-searched*, by some fucking "matron" in a room, and is vio . . . Hold on, and is *violated* . . . physically *violated* . . . By, what *is* it? A "cavity" search. *Why?* Looking for *what*, Dave? That's *my* question. Because, hold the fuck on, because she fit some "profile"? No. Because She Was Associated With *Me.* "How" do I know? Because the same people, who, essentially *raped* her, went and leaked the story to the press. Upon whose orders, Dave? Who would that be? The feds have no horse in this race. It's this *fuckin'* Kid, who thinks his shit don't stink. What did I *do* to him?

(Pause.)

I didn't and I *don't* support him.

(Pause.)

'Cause he's a *fool*.

Is that a crime now? Because I don't vote for this "Man of the People." Was he *always* this . . . DON'T TELL ME HE'S NOT DOING IT. *Because he is.* Was he always this sly, Dave? Where did he *learn* this? In the *ivy-covered halls*? I thought, all he learned there, was to make *scented candles*. What does he think, *politics*, is one of his charming Native *crafts*? He's going to teach us to *weave*? Because I'm in the *opposition*? Look, look, I bounced him on my knee, he went the *other way*, and you went *with* him. That's fine. I *get* it. But might you *explain* to him, I'm *not* his *enemy*. I'm just on the *other side*, and if there *is* no other sss— there is no ballg . . .

(Pause.)

Who knew the girl was on the plane, Dave? Who knew the girl was on the plane? Okay. He needs to make a show about my taxes, that's fine. Here's the thing, how was he brought up? To bring in a woman, who happens to be my fiancée. But if she were not . . . some innocent girl. Who further is under my protection? Does this mean nothing to him? Where'd he get it? From that fucking "man" he married, who . . . No, go ahead and tell him . . . Who, for all her *commie bullshit* is living off both the wealth and the influence her husband inherited. And thrilled to get it. And the nice *fieldstone house* on the Vineyard, and the pied-à-terre in town, and the unions in the *family pouch*, for sixty years. Now he's the *long-lost motherfucker* come down to walk among us. My question? Where did all this money come from? To buy him this "enlightenment," to "lead the oppressed," and he . . .

(He picks up the newspaper.)

(Reads) ". . . parked cars and carried groceries throughout his teenage years." He *did*? The little cocksucker. Two terms of his *share the wealth*, and then I want to see *him* fly commercial. This *hypocrite*.

(Pause.)

You and me stole some horses, Dave. The Old Man died, you went with the Kid. Whoever complained of that? But his *father* would of *called* me. If he had to make a show. "I'm fair game"? All right. But my fiancée is not. His actions are disgraceful, and he wants to fuck with me— there's gonna be a twister in a trailer park . . . Tell me you're kidding. "How?" "How is he fucking with me?"

(He picks up the newspaper again.)

(Into phone; reads) To oppose "malefactors of *great and unearned wealth*" . . . Who would that be? "I, like my father, have devoted my life to public service." Well, but how did they get rich, then? How does that work? With their summer house. Where Steven is raising . . . *(Reads)* "Little Sam and Lisa. To sail four-meter boats, and ride horses in the *evening surf*"? How did they get that money, Ruby? Anybody *care*? 'Cause I see in his ads . . .

(He unfolds the newspaper.)

(Into phone) . . . the *happy family*, 'round the rustic hearth. Whose stones, I recall, came from *England*, at the suggestion of, I believe, some decorator. Who, oh wait, also redid the statehouse. Oh, that was "put to rest"? Wait, *I* remember that stone fireplace. No. All right. No, not because of how it was paid for, but for what it was used

for. Autumn nights, burned a lot of beautiful wood there. *Maple* . . . Applewood . . . What *else* did we burn there? Ruby? When the Old Man begged me? When he held. The hem of my coat.

(Pause.)

What did we burn there?

(Pause.)

I hope that it burned thoroughly, as I hate to leave things lying about.

(Pause.)

You still there? You ever clean out your desk? Something? Back in there, a piece of paper . . . "What is that?" You throw it out. Next week? Invariably. You find that you need it.

(Pause.)

"I'm playing with fire"? What is he going to do to me? I'm cashing out. "And go where?" Wherever I want. You see. And sit around with my wife, whom you thought good to physically abuse.

(Pause.)

What does the Kid *want*, the end of the day?

(Pause.)

He "doesn't want *anything*"? Don't tell me that. 'Cause if he don't want something from me, he wants to do something *to me*. And, I can't let him do that.

(Pause.)

Well, I want something from *him*. I want him to leave me and my friend the fuck alone.

(Pause.)

"Or what?" Or I will put an asterisk next to his name, in the record books. That small pointed star. *You* know what it means? It means *disgrace*. And I will shame this little pimp so badly his children will change their names. Good talking to you.

(He hangs up.)

(To Carson) Go down to the office. In the safe. I need you to fetch me some files.

TWO

The apartment. Morning.

Coffee service on a tray on the table. An overnight bag, open, sits next to it. Mickey enters from a room off to the side. He is carrying a Dopp kit, and puts it into the bag. He opens a newspaper, which is sitting next to the breakfast tray, and reads.

There is a knock on the door.

MICKEY: Yes, come in.

(Carson enters carrying some files.)

Well, I had a vision. An old man. His obligations are met. He takes a young wife. And retires. To a new life. This new life, you might say, is just the ultimate fantasy of wealth: that success, can buy simplicity. But. It is not a fantasy, this new life. One may have it. But one must abandon the old. In which process I was involved. During which I went and acted like a fool. And dragged myself back. When all I had to do was walk away. No. I don't need the files.

CARSON: What would you like me to do with them?

MICKEY: Would you please get me Ms. Pierson?

(Carson dials a phone.)

(Looks at his watch) Have her picked up, at the Choate Hotel, and taken to Flight Services, in Toronto.

CARSON *(Into phone)*: Ms. Ann Black. Hello?

MICKEY: Call Aerstar. I'll take their plane with thanks. It's not their fault.

CARSON *(To Mickey)*: Right away, sir. *(He hands him the phone)*

MICKEY *(Into phone)*: Hello? *(To Carson)* Thank you. *(Into phone)* Hello. *Frankie?* How are you this morning? You see the *Queen* up there? She out today? Well, she goes there *sometimes*. And the Mounties? Yeah. They Always Get Their Man.

(Pause.)

Just like *you*. That's right. Thank God.

(Pause.)

No. No. Don't worry about *anything*.

(Pause.)

'Cause there's nothing to worry ab . . . *(To Carson, gesturing at the coffee, offering him some)* . . . They brought in some coffee.

CARSON: No thank you.

(Mickey points to the coffee service. Carson picks up the tray, and exits.)

MICKEY *(Into phone)*: Yes. Yesterday was a bad day, and we're going to let it go. Isn't that what *you* always advise?

(Pause.)

Well, that's what we're going to do. And our trip? I'm *reminded* that it's called "a honeymoon." Zat too corny for you?

(Pause.)

We'll get married in *London*.

(Pause.)

You're shook up, of course you're shook up.

(Pause.)

No. Here's why. Because I've been through it. Babe, it's just "The Old Life." Reaching out to drag one back. We're going to walk away.

(Pause.)

"How did I get so wise?" Because I'm old enough to be your father. *(Pause. He laughs)* . . . France? You kiss your mom with that same *mouth*? *Where* did you learn those *words*? Talk that way to *me*? *I'm* almost a *married man* . . . "Don't *worry*." It's just some *old friends* down here wanted to play Ringolevio. But I ain't playing.

(Pause.)

Tell you *later*. I'm gonna fly up there, I'll see you in . . . *(He checks his watch)* Three hours.

(Pause.)

The *green card*, babe, is not an issue. Because, *one*: they *took* you off the plane, you did not *leave* the . . .

(Pause.)

"Two?" *Two* is: *should* they mess with us, we'll take our football and *go home*, and you won't *need* a green . . .

(Pause.)

Tahiti, wherever you say, Saint-Estèphe? *Hold* on, you know what we'll be? "Jet-setters." You ever hear that term? Howz *that* sound?

(Pause.)

As of *now*. All I wanna do's have some fun. The "other" *thing*? It isn't fun anymore.

(Pause.)

"Is it because of *you*?" Babe: *everything's* because of you. I love you. You know what we'll have in London? A roast fowl and half a bottle of mulled claret. With, what do they put in it? "Nutmeg" is that an aphrodisiac?

(Pause.)

I dunno either.

(Pause.)

"Ringolevio?" It's a *game* we used to play.

(Pause.)

Well, you *can't* learn it.

(Pause.)

'Cause you have to learn it in the *streets*. Cheer *up*. I'll see you at the airport.

(Pause.)

You, too.

(He hangs up. Carson reenters.)

I'll tell you what: I'm getting *old*. Walking away with the brass ring and the pretty girl, and I went and made a fellow mad. Ain't *that* tempting fate? . . .
CARSON: Do you believe in fate?
MICKEY: Yeah, no. I don't "believe" in it, I just *seen* it.

(Pause.)

All right, let's mend some *fences*. Our friend, the young *governor*, what does he want? He wants to put me in the stocks.
CARSON: For what crime?
MICKEY: Oh no, no. For no "crime"—he needs an issue . . .
Wants to get the cookie jar, and go save the people. How he would *know* "the people," is beyond me, as the only time he ever saw them, they were waxing his car . . . Well, he always *was* a disappointment.

CARSON: To the Old Governor?

MICKEY: To us all.

CARSON: Is he going to win?

MICKEY: There's a lot of foolish people out there—many of them vote.

(Mickey gestures to the files Carson brought in.)

You read the files?

CARSON: No, sir.

MICKEY: Why not?

CARSON: So that, if asked, I may say I didn't read them.

MICKEY: Who would ask you?

CARSON: I don't know. That's why I didn't read them.

MICKEY: Good for you. The Old Man taught "first rule." Never look in the envelope.

CARSON: That was the first rule?

MICKEY: It was up there. F'you meet, maybe one man like that in your life . . .

CARSON: And you were his protégé.

MICKEY: Well, perhaps I was.

CARSON: Of *course* you were.

MICKEY: Yes, of course I was. Last night, in the midst of righteous fury, I thought, What would the Old Man advise.

CARSON: What was the answer?

MICKEY: His answer was, "Think again: a man has the right to change his mind."

CARSON: "It's a *woman's* prerogative to change her mind."

MICKEY: The Old Man said, "It's *anyone's* prerogative . . ." "A *woman* or a *witness*. Or a *judge* . . ."

CARSON: "Or" a judge? . . .

MICKEY: D'you come here to learn Business, Carson?

CARSON: Yes, sir, I did.

MICKEY: Want to know a "secret"?

CARSON: Yes, please.

MICKEY: *Everyone wants something.* What do they want? Money. Judge is no different than anyone else.

CARSON: The Old Governor would bribe a judge?

MICKEY: He was in bed with more judges than Miss America.

CARSON: How did he know that he could trust them?

MICKEY: He *assumed* that he could trust them, till they got a better offer. Just like a car. You put fuel in the tank, you assume it's going to run. Fuel starts to run down, you better top it off.

CARSON: Can anyone be trusted?

MICKEY: That's the question of the Sphinx—

CARSON: And what would the Sphinx say?

MICKEY: Sphinx says, You have to trust *someone*; who'd want to live in *that* world?

CARSON: . . . But sometimes you're wrong.

MICKEY: That's part of the cost of doing business. Point *is*, as the Old Man said, Keep the costs as low as possible. You would have liked him. Hard to fool. Can you imagine what it did, to him; that his son believed the crap we used to tell the voters? Sent his kid to college. Learned to despise the money his dad made to send him there. From nothing. Do you understand? His father? Went out there with nothing? . . .

CARSON: As *you* did.

MICKEY: Carson, I got a *girl* to rub my back.

CARSON: Aren't you entitled to admiration?

MICKEY: I have no fuckin' idea. But you are correct—the response to a compliment is, "Thank you."

(Pause.)

Thank you.

CARSON: You're welcome.

MICKEY: Well. There you *go* . . .

CARSON: What did you used to tell the voters?

MICKEY: The voters. We used to croon to them.

CARSON: What did you croon?

MICKEY: Savage rhythmic chants. To induce a state of unreason. Otherwise called "political awareness."

CARSON: What were the savage chants?

MICKEY: We called them slogans and promises.

(Pause.)

Two things you need, to win an election, Carson: a shitload of money, and a magic phrase . . .

CARSON: Is that what an "issue" is?

MICKEY: . . . and the more absurd the phrase the better. Yes, that's exactly what an "issue" is.

CARSON: But people *vote* for them.

MICKEY: People are fools.

CARSON: Is that why they support the governor?

MICKEY: The governor's bottled water. Y'know what bottled water is? It's *water*. And you tell me voters aren't fools? And we all had a lot of fun playing with 'em. But when it ain't fun anymore, it's time to quit.

CARSON: What would be fun?

MICKEY: What do *you* think?

CARSON: "Peace."

MICKEY: And what would "peace" *mean*?

CARSON: Sir?

MICKEY: Well, see, that's the problem. Maybe we'll learn to "golf." Ms. Pierson and myself.

CARSON: Doesn't Ms. Pierson *play* golf?

MICKEY: Na, she played "field hockey." Things they do in England. Tartan kilts, pretty girls knees, li'l white cotton panties. Maybe I'll learn to knit.

(Pause.)

The Old King.

(Pause.)

The Old King. You see? Cannot find peace, unless he relinquishes his burden—and of course; he cannot.

CARSON: Because?

MICKEY: Because then he's not the King.

CARSON: Yes, of course.

MICKEY: *Now*: the successful man asks, "What *might* I bequeath?" Wisdom? Well, you can't, because it's not transmissible. How about wealth and power? His heir? Misuses the power and squanders the wealth. And the Sea is, once again, Still.

(Pause.)

The Old Man? The Kid? Broke his heart. Went out and broke his father's heart. *You* want the business? . . .

CARSON: You're joking.

MICKEY: I don't know that I *am*.

(Pause.)

CARSON: I . . .

MICKEY: Is the car downstairs?

CARSON: Yes, sir.

MICKEY: Drive out with me, to the airport.

CARSON: Thank you, sir.

MICKEY: Let's have a little talk. Get me Dave Rubenstein, let's patch this up.

(Carson dials a phone.)

(*Referring to the newspaper*) Oh, look, here: "Wicked Despoilers of the Common Wealth . . . and Shirkers of the Communal Burden . . ." You know what *politics* is, Carson? Pawing through shit. Looking for Other People's Money.

(*Pause. Mickey picks up the model of the plane and looks at it.*)

. . . Fuckin' *airplane*. No. I don't need the files. Bad, bad error. Aerstar. Their "loaner" plane. Have 'em pick me up now, in Strafford. I'll fetch Ms. Pierson in Toronto. And then on to London.

(*Mickey picks up the newspaper and reads:*)

"Everything I know I learned from my father . . ."?
CARSON: Is that untrue?
MICKEY: His father was a man.

(*Pause.*)

CARSON (*Into phone*): Mr. Ross for Mr. Rubenstein.

(*He hands the phone to Mickey.*)

MICKEY (*Into phone*): Dave I just realized something. I'm too old for the game. My boy or your boy, finally, what does it matter?

(*Pause.*)

I'm calling you to beg your pardon. Yesterday, I said some things, in anger, which were both untrue, and hurtful. And which I heartily regret. I said things, of which I am ashamed. I've grown old, it seems and have lost control of my speech. I'm going to take it as a sign.

(Pause.)

Out of business, yes, and out of politics.

(Pause.)

That's right. Out of politics. I'm done.

(Pause.)

'Cause it occurs to me, lately, Dave, that it was just a game. And all those years. I been playing on the house's money . . . had a lot of fun . . . But . . .

(Pause. Another phone rings. Carson answers it.)

CARSON *(Into phone)*: Yes?

(Carson listens and makes notes.)

MICKEY *(Into phone)*: But now I'm cashing out. I'm taking my girl to a *desert island. (Laughs)* Well, my age is the only age at which I now can do it, so there you are. Listen. Ruby: what I said yesterday. About Steven? It was discourteous, and it was wrong. I acted like an arrogant fool. I'm sorry. I wish him well, and I'd appreciate it if you told him so.

(Pause.)

He was upset? . . . No, I'm sure he was upset. I can't take the words back, I wish I could. I can but humbly beg his pardon.

(Pause.)

Thank you.

(Pause.)

Good talking to you, too, Dave.

(Mickey hangs up.)

(Pause. Referring to the files) Get this filth out of here. It's bad luck. Call *Henry*, tell him to pay the tax.

(Mickey begins closing up his overnight bag.)

Tell Ms. Pierson, we'll be in Toronto . . .

(Pause.)

What?
CARSON *(Hanging up the phone)*: Aerstar's canceled the plane.
MICKEY: Which plane?
CARSON: Their standby plane.
MICKEY: Tell me again.
CARSON: Aerstar has withdrawn their offer of the standby plane.
MICKEY: What reason did they give?
CARSON: They . . .

(Pause.)

MICKEY: Get Henry on the phone.

(Carson dials the phone.)

What exactly did they say?

(Pause.)

Carson?

CARSON: "Aerstar regrets we are unable to . . ." *(Into phone)* Hello? Mr. Ross for Mr. Abrams . . . *(To Mickey)* ". . . legally supply for Mr. Ross's use . . ." *(Into phone)* Hello? . . .

(Mickey takes the phone.)

MICKEY *(Into phone)*: Hello, *Henry. (To Carson)* "Legally"?
CARSON: Yes, sir.
MICKEY *(Into phone)*: *Henry, Aerstar*, offered me *gratis*, use of one of their planes. No, hold on, and *lemme* talk: they've now withdrawn the offer of . . . You *know* they withdrew? . . . *How* do you know? *(Into phone)* What? Henry, *what?* You received *what?*

(Pause.)

I don't underst . . . Hold on: *why* did they cancel the plane? . . .

(He motions to Carson to transcribe the information.)

"Aerstar reports they have been issued an *Information*" . . . what does *that* mean? ". . . on Michael A. Ross, regarding possible violation of the federal . . ." You're *bullshitting* me. An "information"? What does that . . . ?

(Pause.)

Potential *criminal* charges . . . ? *What? What* criminal . . . ?

(Pause.)

But that's *absurd*. On a *tax* . . . *(To Carson)* Get me Dave Rubenstein.

(Carson picks up the other phone and dials.)

(Into phone) On a state *tax* iss . . .
CARSON *(Into phone, speaking quietly)*: Mr. Rubenstein.
MICKEY *(To himself)*: . . . Federal charges . . .

(Mickey hands his phone to Carson and takes the other phone.)

Take it down.

(Carson begins transcribing.)

(Into phone) Dave? *Stop* it. Will you just make it *stop*?

(Pause.)

You *can* st . . . You made the *one* call, you can make the . . . *Don't* tell me you didn't make the cccc . . . You can *right now*. Yes. You *can*. You can "*advise*" the kkk . . . Well, then you fucking *tell* him: The Kid. Wants to Govern the World. He could *start* by Governing *himself*. Calling this *shit storm* down. Why? Because "People are Basically Good." Except anyone. *Works* for a living. Or made a couple *bucks*, or who *opposes* him politically. You tell this little prick. The first million is the hardest. Let's see him start from nothing except the terror of dying *poor*—*then* let him go out there.

(Pause.)

And you can't . . . you can't . . . What the fuck do you *mean*, "You can't be *involved*"? What *are* you but involved . . . What *do* you want? You want money?

(Pause.)

"I can't legally give you money . . ."? Uh-huh . . .

(Pause.)

Hold on.

CARSON: I . . .

MICKEY: Hold *on*. Here it is . . . *(To Carson)* What did I raise in the last election?

CARSON: Raise or give?

(Mickey gestures "write it down." Carson consults his notes and writes.)

MICKEY *(Into phone)*: I will refrain. From raising money for my side. How much, how much money is that the Kid don't have to find . . . ?

(Carson passes him a note.)

(Pause. Into phone) You *know* how much money we raised last time? It's a *fortune*. Well, I'm going to forgo raising anything this time—I'm done.

(Pause.)

You're telling me the Kid would turn his back on that advantage?

(Pause.)

What does he want? He wants that keepsake we spoke of, I'll send it to you. I'll send it over *now*.

(Pause.)

Well, then, what in the name of God *does* he want? *(Pause)* An "*issue.*"

(Pause.)

An *issue*. Thank you for your frankness.

(He hangs up.)

(To Carson) What?

(Pause.)

Carson.

(Pause.)

What is it?

CARSON: They are indicting you for violation of the Foreign Corrupt Practices Act.

(Pause.)

MICKEY: Give me the phone.

(Mickey takes the phone.)

(Into phone) Henry. The Foreign Corrupt Pract . . . *What* corrupt pract . . . A *bribe*? Whom, *whom* did I "*bribe*"? I . . . "The improvements on the plane, I *paid* for . . . . . . the *permits*"? I'm sure I paid for those, *too*.

(Pause.)

"A special exemption"? For *whom*? "Ms. Pierson"? They purchased an exemption for Ms. Pierson, why? "So she could work on the plane." Why would she need an ex . . . ? "As a Foreign National. She required a special license"?

(Pause.)

And they paid someone off? To get it . . . Aerstar? This exemption? They paid someone off?

(Pause.)

Did they?

(Pause.)

. . . They *admitted* to it? Well, then, that's *their* . . . "It's not a crime for them, but it's a crime for *me*"? *Why? I* never authorized . . . Well, then, wait . . .

(Pause.)

"Under U.S. law . . ."

(Pause.)

Hold on: this motherfucker? You *tell* him, if he wants to take the gloves off, if that's what he wants, he's going to call down hell. Because, remind him, I was *there*. When his father *begged* me.

(Pause.)

Weeping. Weeping, Henry—holding on to my coat. The statute has run and they can't charge the Kid, but I will kill his campaign *dead,* and his "supporters" will turn from him in *disgust.* DOESN'T HE *KNOW* THAT?

(Pause.)

Frankie? What *about* Frankie?

(Pause.)

Wait, wait, "Canada *what*"? "Canada may deport her"? To . . . ? "To the U.S." Why? They aren't after *her*, they . . .

(Pause.)

Don't tell me that.

(Pause.)

Henry. To "*indict*" her . . . ?

(Pause.)

No, they aren't. *What?*

(Pause.)

"To indict her as a 'co-conspirator.'"

(Pause.)

What, what is her position, as a Foreign National?

(Pause.)

"I shouldn't *discuss* it"? With *you*? I shouldn't discuss it with you . . . What do you *mean*? I . . .

(Pause.)

"As it could be construed as perpetuating a . . ."

(Pause.)

"Perpetuating a conspiracy." *What* fucking consp . . . With whom?

(Pause.)

Frankie . . . ?

(Pause.)

And? And what? What do you *mean*, "Stay *away* from her."

(Pause.)

Until *what*? She's my . . . Are you *crazy*? I can't leave her alone up there. *(Looks at his watch)* I'm going up there *now*.

(Pause.)

"My passport"? What about my passport?

(Pause.)

They've pulled my passport? No they haven't.

(Pause.)

Why?

(Pause.)

"As a flight risk."

(Pause.)

Uh-huh . . .

(Pause.)

Well—that would mean they're coming to *arrest* me. Is that . . . ?

(Pause.)

CARSON: I . . .
MICKEY: . . . Are they coming to arrest me?
CARSON: I . . .
MICKEY *(To Carson)*: Just . . . just a moment. *(Into phone)* The Foreign Corrupt Practices Act. What does it carry?

(Pause.)

You're joking.

(Pause.)

Five million dollars and twenty years.

(Pause.)

Twenty years *mandatory*.

(Pause.)

Then I can't plead and bargain. Is that rrr . . .

(Pause.)

I said, "I can't plea-bargain"?
CARSON: Sir . . .
MICKEY *(To Carson)*: Please, please don't speak for a moment.
I *can't* . . .
CARSON: I . . .
MICKEY: *STOP. FOR ONE MOMENT. PLEASE.*

(Pause. Into phone:)

Henry. Can they make it stick?

(Pause.)

Uh-huh.

(Pause.)

Will they grant bail?

(Pause.)

"Under no circumstances . . ." Well, that means while we
fight, I'm going to be in jail . . . Is that right? *(To Carson)*
Get me Dave Rubenstein. *(Into phone)* It's not the feds, it's
the governor. The feds will do as he suggests.

(Pause.)

Because they think he's going to win.
CARSON *(Into the other phone)*: Mr. Ross for Mr. Rubenstein.

MICKEY: Henry, I have to call you back.

(He hangs up.)

CARSON *(Into phone)*: One moment please. *(Pause. To Mickey)* He's on the phone.

(He hands the phone to Mickey.)

MICKEY *(Into phone)*: Dave . . .

(Pause.)

Dave? Well.

(Pause.)

Thank you for taking my call. I very much appreciate it. Dave? I'm sorry we had words. I truly am. The years we spent together. And I'm truly sorry I maligned the governor. His anger at me was fully justified. Would you please tell him I said so? And I thank you keeping the channels open.

(Pause.)

"You can't keep them open anymore."

(Pause.)

Of course you can't. No. No. I understand, it's out of your hands. I *wonder* though, and then I'll let you go, if you'd listen to me. For a moment, if you would.

(Pause.)

Dave. I've been wrong. I've been a fool. And my arrogance has injured. Not just myself. But innocent others. Dave, under my care, who, through no fault of their own . . . I know you don't. But she *is* involved, Dave. And I put her there.

(Pause.)

And I love her.

(Pause.)

Dave, a man who was *wrong* . . . And it doesn't matter if "he overplayed his hand," or however . . .

(Pause.)

If he was wrong.

(Pause.)

When he admits his error. Dave, when he acknowledges himself *wrong*, when he *apologizes*.

(Pause.)

Of course, of *course* there must be a price.

(Pause.)

Well, Dave, you tell me. What would the price be?

(Pause.)

A time for reflection.

(Pause.)

How much time would that be, Dave, to cleanse the error.

(Pause.)

Tell me a number, Dave.

(Pause.)

Two years . . . ?

(Pause.)

Two years.

(Pause.)

And come home to the girl? Who was not involved.

(Pause.)

Dave? Is that right?

(Pause.)

Thank you, Dave.

(Pause.)

May I send you a gift?

(Pause.)

No, God forbid. Just, a souvenir. Of those times we spent by the fire. Thank you, Dave. Thank you very much.

(He hangs up.)

(To Carson) Get me Mr. Abrams.

(He picks up the model plane and examines it.)

(To himself) Little fucking *toy* . . .
CARSON *(Into phone)*: Hello . . . ?

(He hands the phone to Mickey.)

MICKEY *(Into phone)*: *Henry.* The charge will be negotiated down. And I will plead to the lesser charge . . . because Rubenstein just . . .

(Pause.)

I told him the truth, that I'd been a fool, and threw myself upon his mercy.

(Pause.)

Well, he *did* . . .

(Pause.)

Because he's the better man—I don't know. Here's what it is: the girl gets full immunity. In writing. In *writing*, and I'll plead to a felony that carries two years. And I'll serve fourteen months . . .

(Pause.)

On whatever charge he wants. And that's the deal. Ms. Pierson and I are separated for a while and then it's done.

(Pause.)

I want to sit down with you and review Ms. Pierson's situation while I'm gone. No. No, I don't want to come to the office. Can I come to your house, this even . . . No, Henry, it's not the best outcome, but it's the best *possible* outcome.

(Pause.)

Thinking further changes nothing. *(Pause)* I'll see you around eight.

(He hangs up. Pause.)

CARSON: Sir, I'm so sorry.

(Pause.)

MICKEY: Lock the door.

(Pause.)

Go lock the door.

(Carson does so.
   Mickey picks up a pad and pen and writes.)

I want you to leave here, go to this man, and give him *this*.

(Mickey continues writing.)

Get me Ms. Pierson on the phone. We need to get her somewhere safe.

(Carson begins dialing.)

Tell this man to have one of his people, *in* Toronto . . .

CARSON *(Into phone)*: Ms. Ann Black.

MICKEY: Tell him to send a woman. *(He continues writing)* Ms. Pierson is to walk away from everything she has in the hotel. All of her bags. *Everything.* And go with their woman. Out of the hotel. I want her flown from Toronto, to Saint-Estèphe. Right now.

CARSON *(Into phone)*: One moment, please . . .

MICKEY: . . . and *I* need to get out of the country.

CARSON: Your *passport*, sir?

MICKEY: . . . What . . . ?

CARSON: They canceled your passport.

MICKEY: . . . pick an airport. Out of state. *(Of the note)* Tell this man to have a plane meet me there in two hours, Miami— Saint-Estèphe, phony the flight plans. Buy the pilot. Buy the plane, you need to.

CARSON: I don't understand.

MICKEY: What don't you understand?

CARSON: I don't understand why you won't take the deal.

MICKEY: Oh, Carson . . .

CARSON: They . . .

MICKEY: There *is* no deal. He'll have me plead guilty to the lesser charge, then he'll indict me for conspiracy, and I'll die in jail. Isn't that *clear?* That's his *issue.*

CARSON: "That's his issue . . ."

MICKEY: That he "moved against the Great." Transparent corrupt little piece of *shit.* Who does he think he's fucking with?

(He continues writing.)

Ms. Pierson may not want to go. You tell him. Have his operative convince her, *drug* her if they have to. Get her on the plane. You understand?

(Carson does not move.
    Mickey finishes the note and hands it to Carson.)

There you are.

(Pause.)

What?
CARSON: Perhaps you should take the note, sir.

(Pause.)

MICKEY: I'm sorry? . . .
CARSON: I think it might be better if *you* took the note.
MICKEY: Uh-huh. You don't want to take the note.
CARSON: No.

(Pause.)

MICKEY: Well: "There you go . . ."

(Pause.)

No, you're not wrong. This isn't your fight. I beg your pardon.

(Pause.)

CARSON: Sir . . .

MICKEY: Carson?

CARSON: Yes . . .

MICKEY: I understand. You may go.

CARSON: I . . .

MICKEY: I understand. I "absolve" you. All right? You may go.

CARSON: Thank you, sir.

(Pause. Carson starts to exit, holding the files.)

MICKEY: Just leave the files.

CARSON: I'd prefer not to do that, sir.

MICKEY: You'd "prefer not to do that"?

CARSON: Yes, that's right.

MICKEY: Are you a thief?

CARSON: No.

MICKEY: No, I don't think so, but then why would you take my property?

(Pause.)

Just tell me.

CARSON: They can charge me with conspiracy.

MICKEY: Well, anyone can charge you with anything. But what conspiracy have you been part of? Carson? There *is* no consp . . .

CARSON: . . . And you said you were going to trade these files, for imm . . .

MICKEY: *What* did I say . . . ?

CARSON: For *immunity* . . .

MICKEY: No, I never said that. No, you may have "understood" that. *Incorrectly.* But I never said those words. I *said* I was sending Mr. Rubenstein a *gift*. Were those the words I said?

CARSON: Yes.

MICKEY: So why are you taking my property?

CARSON: You threatened, to blackmail the governor . . .

MICKEY: I did? With *what*?

CARSON: With what the files contain.

MICKEY: How would you know what they contain?

(Pause.)

CARSON: I read the files.

(Pause.)

MICKEY: Ah huh. Of course you did.

(Pause.)

Well now you know who you're dealing with.

CARSON: I know who *you're* dealing with.

MICKEY: All right. But, you're jammed up, too. You stuck your nose under the tent, and now you're frightened. And legitimately so. The question is: Where does your safety lie? Your safety lies with me. Why? Because if you go to *them* . . .

CARSON: I cannot be party to a criminal act.

MICKEY: Taking the files from me is a crime, Carson, they're my property. They *belong* to me.

CARSON: I won't break the law.

MICKEY: Then don't. For if you turn on me? Carson? And go to them, if that's your plan. And lie—and they'll make you lie—that's perjury. Which is a terrible crime. To swear away someone's life.

(Pause.)

So *you* tell *me*.

(Pause.)

CARSON: I'm frightened.

MICKEY: I know you are, and I'll protect you. How? With money, 'cause that's all there is. You want some? Here's a check. *(He signs a check)* You fill it in. You'll need it. You deserve it.

(Pause.)

Yes . . . ?

CARSON: How can I walk away from my *life?*

MICKEY: Carson. Your life is *done* here. Do you understand.

CARSON: But I've done nothing wrong.

MICKEY: Neither has Ms. Pierson, and they're trying to destroy *her.* What are they going to do to *you?* But. Like her, listen to me, *you will be* protected.

(Pause.)

CARSON: What have you done to me?

MICKEY: I've done nothing to you, Carson, and I'm out of time. I've got to move. If I had the time I could sit *down* and . . .

CARSON: No. I will not go to jail for you.

(Mickey picks up the phone and dials.)

MICKEY: But I swear to you . . . *(Into phone)* Ann Black . . . *(To Carson)* If . . . *(Into phone)* Miss Ann Black. *(To Carson)* I swear to you, I will take care of you.

CARSON: I can't . . .

MICKEY: Carson, I owe you. And I *will* repay your loyalty. The other guy, you go to him, all you can do is pray. 'Cause you've got nothing to trade. *(Into phone)* Hello, Frankie.

Frankie. There's been a change in plans . . . no . . . no
one . . . Frankie? Fr . . . no one is going to harm you.
Would I ever let that happen? Fr . . . Frankie. I Will Never
Let Anyone Harm You.

(Pause.)

. . . Frankie, no one *can* harm you. No one knows where
you *are*.

CARSON: I know where she is.

MICKEY *(To himself)*: . . . Oh no . . .

CARSON: I . . .

MICKEY: You don't want to do that, son.

CARSON: I know where she is.

MICKEY *(To himself)*: . . . No.

CARSON: And I'm going to propose a trade.

(Pause.)

I said I'm proposong a trade.

MICKEY: I heard you.

(Pause.)

CARSON: Give yourself up and I'll let the girl go free.

MICKEY *(Into phone)*: Frankie. Yes. Hold . . . Frankie, hold on.
(To Carson) That's the trade—I surrender, and, "You'll let
the girl go free . . ."

CARSON: It's a simple proposition.

MICKEY: Of course. How does it work?

CARSON: I tell Mr. Rubenstein that I'm bringing you in.

MICKEY: . . . Go on.

CARSON: Then you can make whatever plans you want. For
the girl.

(Pause.)

There's no more information.

MICKEY: Well, then. It must be time to make up my mind.

(Pause.)

CARSON: It is.

(Pause.)

MICKEY: All right.

CARSON: All right, to *what?*

MICKEY: You make the call. To Mr. Rubenstein. And I'll give myself up.

CARSON: I'm sorry.

(Pause.)

MICKEY: Huh? You're "sorry"?

CARSON: Yes. I truly am. But I think . . . I think that it's possible—

(Carson begins reaching for a phone.
  Mickey picks up the metal model of the plane, and begins beating Carson with it.
  Carson starts screaming.
  There is a knocking on the door.
  Pause.
  Carson falls screaming.
  Mickey continues beating the fallen Carson, who is now silent.
  The knocking grows louder.
  Pause.
  Mickey listens to the knocking.
  Mickey begins screaming.)

MICKEY: HELP ME.

(Mickey goes around the apartment knocking over furniture and lamps while screaming.)

STAY AWAY FROM ME. He's *cut* me . . . He's going to kill me . . .

(Mickey takes a piece of the battered metal plane and begins gashing his flesh with it. The blood flows.)

Help me. Will . . . Will . . . Oh my God. Will no one help an old *man* . . . ?

END

DAVID MAMET's numerous plays include *Oleanna*, *Glengarry Glen Ross* (winner of the Pulitzer Prize and New York Drama Critics' Circle Award), *American Buffalo*, *Speed-the-Plow*, *Boston Marriage*, *November*, *The Anarchist* and *Race*. He wrote the screenplays for such films as *The Verdict*, *The Untouchables* and *Wag the Dog*, and has twice been nominated for an Academy Award. He has written and directed ten films, including *Homicide*, *The Spanish Prisoner*, *State and Main*, *House of Games*, *Spartan* and *Redbelt*. In addition, he wrote the novels *The Village*, *The Old Religion*, *Wilson* and many books of nonfiction, including *Bambi vs. Godzilla: On the Nature, Purpose and Practice of the Movie Business*; *Theatre*; *Three Uses of the Knife: On the Nature and Purpose of Drama* and the *New York Times* bestseller *The Secret Knowledge: On the Dismantling of American Culture*. His HBO film *Phil Spector*, starring Al Pacino and Helen Mirren, aired in 2013. He was co-creator and executive producer of the CBS television show *The Unit*. He is a founding member of the Atlantic Theater Company.